W9-ACW-611

TAKE A CLOSER LOOK AT YOUR

Ears

BY JENNY FRETLAND VANVOORST

The Child's World®

Published by The Child's World®
1980 Lookout Drive • Mankato, MN 56003-1705
800-599-READ • www.childsworld.com

Acknowledgments
The Child's World®: Mary Berendes, Publishing Director
Red Line Editorial: Editorial direction and production
The Design Lab: Design
Content Consultant: Jeffrey W. Oseid, MD

Photographs ©: Photodisc, 5, 6, 24; Jean Valley/
Shutterstock Images, 7; Shutterstock Images, 9, 10, 15,
20; Leonello Calvetti/Shutterstock Images, 12; Alila Sao
Mai/Shutterstock Images, 14; Paul Matthew Photography/
Shutterstock Images, 16; Kalmatsuy Tatyana/Shutterstock
Images, 17, 23; Alex Luengo/Shutterstock Images, 18;
iStockphoto/Thinkstock, 19

Front cover: Sukhonosova Anastasia/Shutterstock Images;
Kalmatsuy Tatyana/ Shutterstock Images; Shutterstock
Images

ISBN: 978-1623235451
LCCN: 2013931454

Printed in the United States of America
Mankato, MN
July, 2013
PA02175

About the Author

Jenny Fretland VanVoorst is a writer and editor of books for young people. She enjoys learning about all kinds of topics and has written books that range in subject from ancient peoples to artificial intelligence. When she's not reading and writing, Jenny enjoys kayaking, playing the piano, and watching wildlife. She lives in Minneapolis, Minnesota, with her husband, Brian, and their two pets.

Table of Contents

CHAPTER 1

Listening to Your Ears

Our world is made up of sounds. Some sounds are soft and give us comfort. Other sounds are loud and warn us of danger. But we would not hear these sounds without our ears. Ears are a part of the **auditory system**. This is the body system that helps us hear. The ears catch **sound waves** and turn them into messages the brain can understand.

Sound waves become the purr of a cat or the honk of a car horn. When you listen to music or your friend's funny story, your brain **decodes** sound waves. This is called hearing. Our ears are two of the most important parts of our body because they allow us to hear. Hearing is one of our most important senses. Being able to hear helps us speak and listen to others.

Loud sounds can be too harsh for our ears.

Look in the mirror. You have an ear on either side of your head. Earlobes are the fatty part at the bottom of your ears. Each ear helps you tell where sound waves are coming from. See how your ears are cup-shaped and face forward? They act like a funnel to trap and focus sound waves.

Some people's earlobes connect to their head, while others are separated. Which do you have?

Her earlobes are connected to her head.

The part of your ear you can see is called the **outer ear**. The outer ear is only a small part of your ear. The parts that turn the sound waves into messages for your brain are inside.

Some ear parts help you keep your balance. In one part of your **inner ear**, fluid moves in tubes. The way the fluid moves around helps your brain understand the way your body is moving. The brain sends messages to the muscles to keep you from falling over. Without balance, you wouldn't be able to ride a bike without training wheels.

Balance is what helps you walk on a balance beam.

CHAPTER 2

How Ears Work

Let's follow the path a sound wave takes to your brain. Imagine your teacher has called your name. Your name comes out of her mouth as a sound wave. The wave travels through the air to your ear. The outer ear funnels the wave inside to the middle part of your ear. This part is called the **middle ear**. There, the sound wave travels through a narrow tube until it reaches the **eardrum**.

The eardrum acts like the top of a drum. When sound waves hit the eardrum, the eardrum **vibrates**. The vibrations move through three tiny bones in your middle ear.

The middle ear is a space smaller than a little piece of candy.

The three bones in your middle ear are called the hammer, the anvil, and the stirrup. They are the tiniest bones in the human body. They make the sound waves bigger so you can hear them. The three bones move vibrations into the inner ear. Then the vibrations enter a tube called the **cochlea**. The cochlea is filled with liquid.

The cochlea is curled up in a spiral shape like a snail's shell.

The cochlea has tiny hairs inside. The vibrations move the liquid over the hairs. When the hairs move, they send a message to the brain. The brain decodes this message, and it becomes a sound. You know this sound as your name. You also know it was your teacher who spoke. And you can tell where she is in the room.

Have you ever felt sick to your stomach while riding in a car? Motion sickness happens when your ears send messages to the brain that don't match the messages your other senses send.

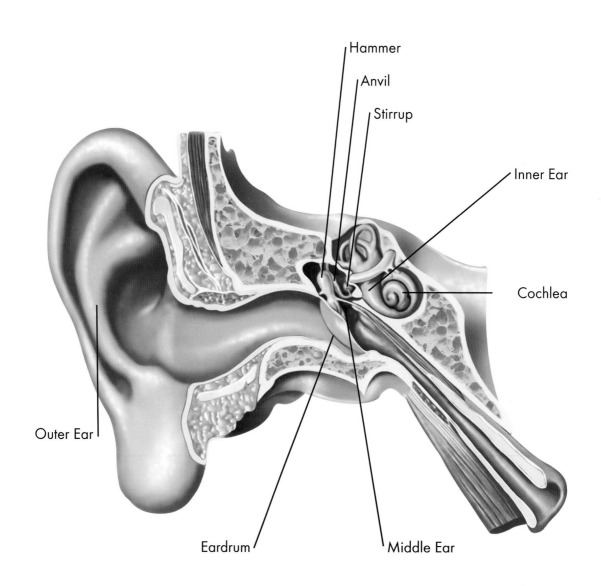

Hammer

Anvil

Stirrup

Inner Ear

Cochlea

Outer Ear

Eardrum

Middle Ear

Have you ever listened to a recording of your voice and thought it didn't sound like you? When you speak, your outer ear catches the sound waves. The sound waves also travel directly through your head to reach your inner ear.

Your voice sounds deeper to you than it does to others because you hear sound waves from both parts of your ear. Record yourself talking to hear how you sound to others. When you listen to the recording, you will only hear the sound waves your outer ear picks up.

CHAPTER 3

When Ears Don't Work

Our ears do a great job helping us listen to people and hear sounds. But ears don't always work as they should. Ear infections happen when **germs** get stuck in the different parts of the ear. Fluid can then get trapped in the middle ear. Your middle ear traps the fluid to try to help fight away the germs. But all of the fluid makes your ears hurt, and it can make it hard to hear.

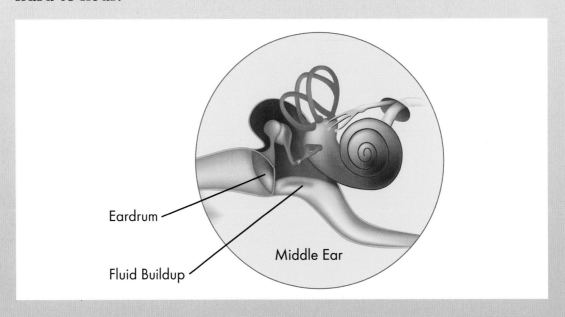

Eardrum

Fluid Buildup

Middle Ear

Medicine can help fix most ear infections. But people who get a lot of ear infections may need an operation. A doctor will put small tubes inside the ear to help drain the fluid out.

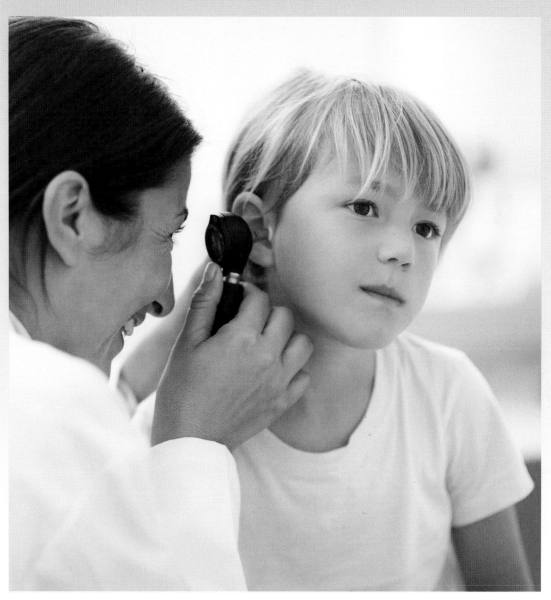

During a checkup, an otoscope is used to see inside your ears.

As we get older, we can start to lose our hearing. The loud noises we hear can damage the inner ear. When sound waves travel across the hairs in the inner ear, they bend the hairs like grass bends in the wind. Over time, the hairs can stay bent. If the hairs are bent over, they can't move to send a message to the brain. Hearing aids can help people of all ages hear more sounds.

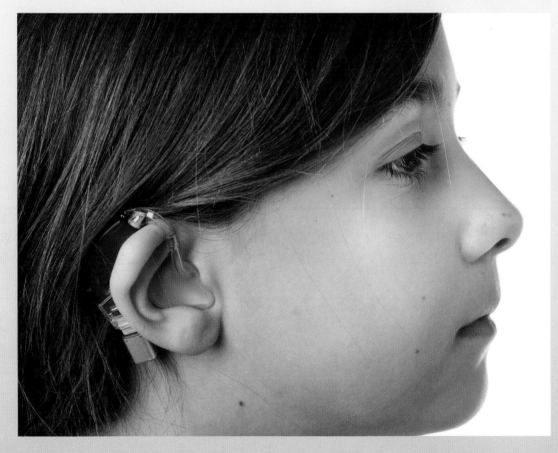

Hearing aids make sound waves larger so they can reach the brain.

To hear better, just use your hands. Cup your hand behind your ear and listen.

Your hands can help pick up sound and funnel it straight into your ear.

CHAPTER 4
Taking Care of Your Ears

Ears can take care of themselves. One of the ways they do this is by making earwax. Earwax is made by **glands** in the outer ear. This sticky wax traps dust and other small particles before they get inside the ear.

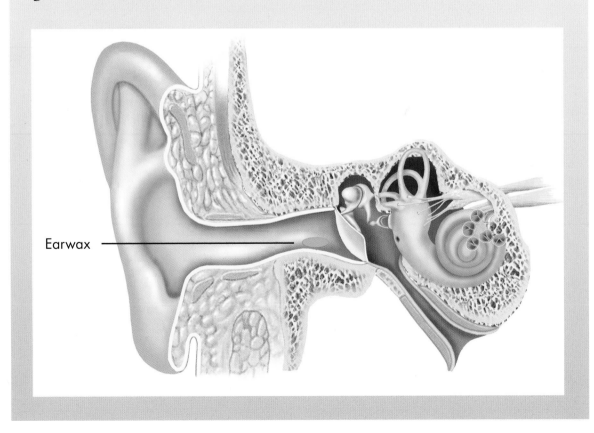

Earwax

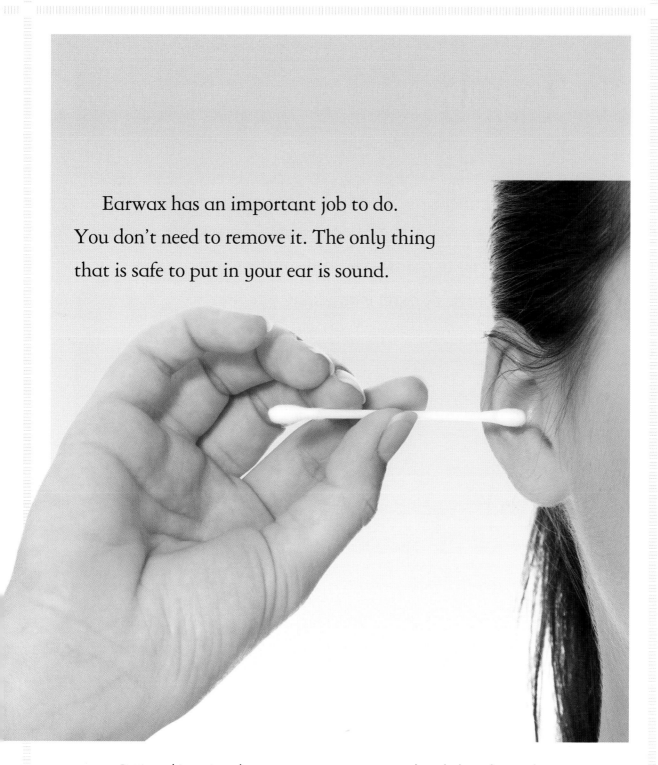

Earwax has an important job to do. You don't need to remove it. The only thing that is safe to put in your ear is sound.

Putting objects into the ear to remove wax can poke a hole in the eardrum.

There are some ways you can help keep your ears healthy. Most importantly, protect your ears when you are around loud noises, such as the sound of a lawn mower. Earplugs can help protect your ears from sounds that are too loud.

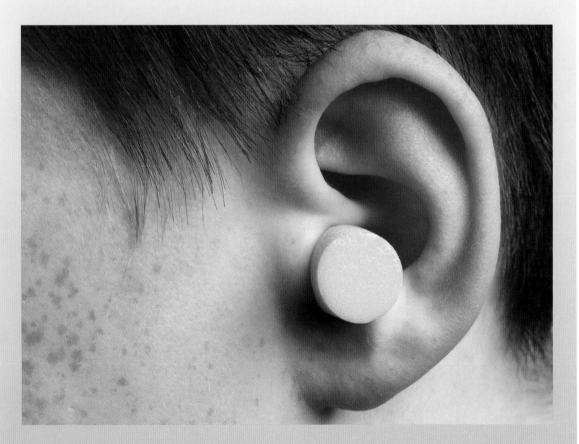

If you plan on being around loud noises, be sure to have a pair of earplugs handy.

Be gentle with your ears. Protect them when you have a cold by blowing your nose softly. A strong blow can push germs up into your middle ear where they can cause an infection.

Your ears never stop working. The ears hear sounds while you sleep, but the brain shuts them out.

Your ears help you stay connected to other people and the world around you. Take care of your ears so you can enjoy your dog's bark and your sister's laugh. Be good to your ears, and they will be good to you.

GLOSSARY

auditory system (aw-di-TOR-ee sis-tuhm) The auditory system is the body system that allows us to hear. The outer ear is the only part of the auditory system we can see.

cochlea (KAHK-lee-uh) The cochlea is a hollow tube in the inner ear. The cochlea changes sound waves into messages so the brain can identify a sound.

decodes (dee-KODEZ) Something decodes when it changes information into something that is easier to understand. The brain decodes sound waves the ears pick up.

eardrum (EER-druhm) The eardrum is a thin piece of skin in the ear. The eardrum vibrates when hit by sound waves, which makes us hear the sound.

germs (jurmz) Germs are very small living things that can cause disease. Germs that get stuck in the ear can cause an ear infection.

glands (glandz) Organs that make natural chemicals in the body are called glands. Glands in the outer ear make earwax.

inner ear (IN-ur eer) The inner ear is the innermost part of the ear. The inner ear turns sound waves into messages your brain can understand.

middle ear (MID-uhl eer) The middle ear is the part of the ear between the outer ear and inner ear. The middle ear makes sound waves louder as they travel from the outer ear to the inner ear.

outer ear (OU-ter eer) The outer ear is the fleshy part of the ear you can see. The outer ear funnels sound waves into the middle ear.

sound waves (sound wayvz) Waves or series of vibrations in the air are called sound waves. Ears catch sound waves, and the brain turns them into meaning.

vibrates (VYE-brates) Something vibrates when it moves back and forth very fast. The eardrum vibrates when sound waves hit it.

LEARN MORE

BOOKS

Ballard, Carol. *How Your Ears Work.* New York: Gareth Stevens, 2011.

Parker, Steve. *The Senses.* Chicago: Raintree, 2004.

Vogel, Julia. *Your Sensational Sense of Hearing.* Mankato, MN: Child's World, 2011.

WEB SITES

Visit our Web site for links about the ears: **childsworld.com/links**

Note to Parents, Teachers, and Librarians: We routinely verify our Web links to make sure they are safe and active sites. So encourage your readers to check them out!

INDEX